Wayfarer

Poems by Gennet Emery
with illustrations by Ann Hegarty

Star Books Inc.
lifting up the Light of the world
Wilson NC 27893

Library of Congress Cataloging in Publication Data:

Emery, Gennet Maxon.
Wayfarer : poems / by Gennet M. Emery ; art by Ann L. Hegarty.
128 p. cm.
ISBN 0-915541-55-6 : $8.00
1. Christian poetry, American. I. Title.
PS3555.M426W38 1989
811'.54--dc20 89-26354
CIP

Scripture quotations are identified as follows:
KJV = King James Version
NIV = New International Version
RSV = Revised Standard Version
TLB = The Living Bible
Some pronouns not capitalized in the above translations are capitalized in this book.

ISBN: 0-915541-55-6

Published by:

Available From:
Gennet M. Emery
W. 723 Briar Cliff Ct.
Spokane, WA 99218

(919) 237-1591

TABLE OF CONTENTS

TABLE OF CONTENTS
continued

to those whose hands

in mercy and in love

reached down to help

a pilgrim on the way

Nightsounds

Within the deeply shadowed forest
Cascading through the still night air
Break forth the hidden bird's
Pure notes of joy

Although she does not even know
If dawn will come again
Or when
Yet on she sings
To welcome that sweet benison of light

In dark and lonely night travail of soul
O give my spirit grace to sing
Before the dawn

The Lord
turns
my darkness
into light.
2 Samuel 22:29 NIV

Transmutation

With diligence he washed his cup
And brought it to the throne
Presented to the Lord his inner life
And prayed it might be filled
With some small portion from the Lord
So he could be of use

With kindness and in love the answer came –
With gentle hands He took that cup and broke it
Crushed it into dust and ground it fine
Then – needing clay – He mixed that earth
With living flowing water
His very Life and Spirit
Brought the two together
    Man's dust
    His Life
And formed and shaped a vessel to His liking
Then passed it through the leaping fires
Till it was tempered by the flames –
At last made ready for His use
He had what He desired

For now, the needy suppliant
Instead of vainly struggling
To hold the Life of God
Within his meager bowl
By God's own processes and grace
He had become it

How the precious sons of Zion,
once worth their weight in gold,
are now considered as pots of clay,
the work of a potter's hands!
Lamentations 4:2 NIV

Sacrifice

I found it not so hard
To see what had to go
And on my altar heap
My sorry load

Long cherished dreams
Some secret sins
My own desires and will
A selfish plan
And wayward thoughts
A discontent
A questioning

An endless list
And changing every day

But oh, how hard
To light the match
And start the conflagration!

Could You not send a lightning bolt
From heaven's gate?

But no
It is an act of will to make alone

Yet since I find it hard
And oft impossible to do
Enfold my faltering hand
Within Your own
And give it strength to move

. . . Abraham reached out his hand and took the knife
. . . so Abraham called that place
The Lord will provide. . . . Genesis 22:9,14 NIV

Will o' the Wisp

For years You stayed
Just beyond my grasp
Elusive as a firefly
You danced and flitted
On the sunny meadow
In the shady glens
Hid behind the trees
And hovered over flowers
And gave me just a glimpse
Of what You really were

Some times You came so close
I almost touched You
And then on You went
Leaving me with just desire
Clenched within my hands

So long you seemed to be
Beyond my reach
And so I asked
Why, Lord?
Why so many years
I could not see You clear
Or hold You in my hand?

Beloved child
To make you follow

Draw me:
we will
run
after thee.
Song of Solomon 1:4 KJV

Job's Friends

Long desert spaces of the soul
    bleak ribs of life jutting over the sands
The sun bleak too
    its colors spare and thin upon the rocks
    unable to give heat or warmth

Darkness comes
    the air stirs and its cold fingers wrap me
    tightly and I shiver
    here in my extended prison

For if I walk miles in any direction
    I cannot escape
    I cannot reach the edge
    Though I can see it

You laugh and try to bring me out
    and I know you do not see
    nor hear
    nor understand
How to bring warmth and freedom to my soul

O Lord, where is my Elihu?

Miserable
comforters
are
you
all!
Job 16:2 NIV

Fulfillment

God knew
So long before the time
He planted a small tree
Within the wilderness

Alone it grew
And waited

Tap root plunging down
To reach a hidden source of life
And make the leaves branch out
Amidst that desolation

Rooted in the love of God
The wood grew fragrant
And its leaves perfumed
And aromatic was the sap

Alone it grew
And waited

Until the day when Moses came
And wrenched it out
To sacrifice it in the bitter pool
And make the waters sweet to drink

Alone it died
Fulfilled

And the Lord showed him a tree,
and he threw it into the water,
and the water became sweet.
Exodus 15:25 RSV

Anointing: His

A fervent heart of love
prepared her for the act
to take all that she had
and waste it on a gift

Costly nard and flask
and criticized by those
who nothing knew of love
or giving all to Him

A brokenness revealed
a fragrant spirit that
did minister to Him
from shattered grateful heart

A fragrance filled the house
that from her crushing came
prepared by her own loss
and sufferings unknown

Prepared Him for His death
with tender loving hands
a sacrifice so great
yet human, not divine . . .

A woman came
with an alabaster flask . . .
of pure nard,
very costly,
and she broke the flask
and poured it over His head.
Mark 14:3 RSV

Anointing: Hers

He crushed His only Son
and brought Him down in pain
to anguish and to death
and left Him all alone

And as that crushing came
that fragile heart and form
both from within without
was broken riven torn

Salt sweat and tears, dark blood
transfigured as they fell
to sacred costly balm
a cleansing fragrant oil

That sight required she kneel
and reverent bow her head
present her broken life
for mercy's healing flow

God took His loving hand
and broke with tender care
His alabaster flask
and poured it over her

Then the Lord said
. . . "Take myrrh . . . fragrant cinnamon
. . . fragrant cane . . . cassia . . . olive oil.
Make these into . . .
a fragrant blend,
the work of a perfumer.
It will be
the sacred anointing oil."
Exodus 30:23-24 NIV

The Breath of His Spirit

On this cold icicle
Of a heart
Breathe
With the warmth
Of Your spirit
Dissolve
Melt
Undo me
Then take that
Insignificant
Muddied pool
Of my life
And breathe again
Till it becomes
Alive
Pure
Cleansed
That even one day
A fountain
Of living water
May spring up
And streams can flow
A place
Where children play
And weary ones
Become refreshed
Where even You
May take a cup
To quench Your thirst

He breathed on them,
and said to them:
Receive
the Holy Spirit.
John 20:22 RSV

Seaweed

From muddied floor
Of my own sea
Well nourished grew
The weeds – complaint, self pity

Writhed up until
Their tentacles
Wrapped tight around my form
And would not let me go

Remorseless to the end
Their rubbery strength
Drew me deep to drown
In suffocating depths

Today
also
my complaint
is
bitter.
Job 23:2 RSV

Lament for a Child

Some thought the pain was less
Because I never saw you
But oh, I did!
My heart and mind wove textured skin,
Caressed your cheeks, touched finespun hair
And smelled sweet breath

Although you dwelt within my womb
In darkness, secret and unseen
I knew your presence there
A living part of my own flesh
Whose heart was linked to mine

And then you left
Too soon to bear earth's weighted air
And so I silent mourn
My tears as inward as your life
And yet you truly lived
As real as if my arms had felt your weight
And sensed your body's warmth close pressed to mine

So now I raise a stone within my soul
To mark your place
Your name engraved by acid tears
Still carry you in memory's womb
And feel grief's weight in empty arms

So tender were the days you lived with me
Reluctant do I set you free
Yet can I sense a tempered joy
To think you whole, complete,
New-born to breathe a fresher air
In worlds more real than those I know

We wait together, oh my child,
For one day I will reach and find
Your hand within my own
And feeling that embrace
Your kiss upon my cheek
So move from dream into reality
And know a different motherhood at last

David, on the death of his child:
I will
go to him,
but he will
not
return
to me.
2 Samuel 12:23 NIV

Carpenter Shop

Imagine!
That of this knotty stubborn
Gnarled and twisted
Less than common pine
He wants to make His image!

Sawing, carving, gouging,
Chipping, shaping, sanding!
Splinters flying!
Sawdust falling!
Axe and plane and chisel
In steady, firm, insistent hands.

Necessary wounds
To form the likeness
Of the face of Jesus.

Yet at His side a pot of oil
Sits warm upon the fire
With which He heals the wood
Preventing cracks from forming.

Good craftsmen are both strong and gentle.

For He wounds,
but He also binds up;
He injures,
but His hands also heal.
Job 5:18 NIV

Voices on the Wind

He stood confused
Uncertain and bewildered
A little lamb amidst the bleating of the flock
So many voices ringing in his ears

The fearful cries of timid ewes
Wise solemn tones of elder brothers
Some platitudes from portly rams
Rebellious whisperings from the young
Enticing words from wolves disguised as sheep
And even his own voice drowned out the others

So
Deafened by the noise he wandered off
(They called him prodigal, a rebel, loner –
if not a little strange)
And maybe not the wisest thing to do
For out there in the dark
Alone and unattended
He fell into the ditch

Yet in that silent night
Beneath the brilliant stars
Among the rocks and thorns
And shivering in the cold
At last he heard the Shepherd's voice
Strong true and clear upon the wind
Looking for His lamb

So when in time he was brought back
To dwell among his brothers
He always stood
Facing to the wind

I will search for
the lost (sheep)
and bring back
the strays.
I will bind up
the injured
and strengthen
the weak.
Ezekiel 34:16 NIV

The Discipline of Snow

"There is no spring without the snow"
Or so my mother used to say
Yet I would gladly have foregone
The winter seasons of my life

Until I understood the need
For snow to lie upon the ground
That it might melt into the earth
And living water so become

That long white nights of bitter frost
Are best for viewing sparkling stars
Enable bulbs to burst in bloom
And make the sap run in the trees

That cold gray days may be a balm
For too much sparkle hurts the eyes
And still mooned nights can quiet bring
That noisy spring knows nothing of

That cycling freezes with their thaws
Can break the hardest fallow ground
And wintry blasts of frigid air
Make saplings sink their roots deep down

That the thick blanket of the snow
Protects the dormant life beneath
And that in spite of nature's sleep
The birds and rabbits find their food

There is no way ordained by God
In this great paradox of His
That we can truly taste the spring
Without the discipline of snow.

Hast thou
entered into
the treasures
of the snow?
Job 38:22 KJV

Farewell to Winter

The brittle, sere and broken leaves
Go scuttling past in disarray
Flung by the chill November breeze
That brings the winter on its way.

I stand and shiver in the air
While this, my Friend, digs deep a place
Hid in these woods so dark and bare
Where winter holds its chill embrace.

Dig deep, O Friend, this grave for me,
This place in which to lay my past,
For I would fain let memory be,
And rid myself of it at last.

Forget the gathered heap of sorrows,
The tortured labyrinth of thought,
The endless gray and dull tomorrows,
The futile dreams I once had sought.

Toss in the vain and bitter tears,
The foolish wish, the aching heart,
The failures spent of all the years,
Then do Thou set my self apart

To turn away from what I see
Of earthly longings, pride, and shame,
Cast off the chains and set me free
To only look on Jesus' Name.

I turn my back on earth piled high,
Then spirit, soul, and body sing,
An April fragrance drifts on by,
And now I face the coming spring.

For lo,
the winter
is past,
the rain
is over
and gone.
The flowers
appear
on the earth,
the time
of singing
has come.
Song
of
Solomon
2:11-12
RSV

Detour

My wandering footsteps circles made,
Retraced, went off the edge,
A crazy quilted pattern drawn
Upon the unmarked sand.

Yet as He looked down from His throne
With keen, unclouded eyes,
He saw that trail as clear and true
Directed straight towards Him.

So differently He views my life
From my short-sighted gaze,
Take heart, my soul, when gone astray,
He sees the truer end.

But He knows
the way
that I take.
Job 23:10 NIV

Peter

What rises up within
To turn a craven soul
Into God's lion?

The Lamb

They
overcame
him
by
the blood
of
the Lamb.
Revelation 12:11 NIV

Refuge

When I have loved too much
    desired too much
    beyond my lot and God's design
And burnt my fingers
    at fires of my own kindling
    or spent too long at someone else's blaze
What then?

Is there a place remote
    and hidden in the hills
    amidst the snow
    where You have kept a flame alight
Where I may dare approach yet once again
    to shelter from the wind
    and warm my hands and heart?

For in You
I take refuge.
Psalm 16:1 NIV

The Transformed Christ

How beautiful You are, O Man of Sorrows,
Bent low to bear Your load of grief and pain,
Beneath that weighty cross You slip and stumble
And fall as if to never rise again.

From underneath those thorns the blood comes flowing
To mask Your face, Your countenance of woe,
The drops have stained the cobblestones beneath You,
To mark the path Your Father bids You go.

Your eyes reflect the horrors of men's scourgings,
Yet dwell on heaven and the Father's will,
Your exile here on earth is almost ended,
As You ascend that mound, Golgotha's hill.

Your scarred and weathered hands from hours of working
Receive the nails that also pierce Your heart,
Which broken now in two pours forth its anguish
To heaven above, which seems a world apart.

Despised, rejected, bruised, and judged forsaken,
Humiliated, shamed and mocked at will,
An object of contempt, of scorn, of pity,
By cruel men who seek to do You ill.

No form or comeliness draw my attention,
No outward beauty calls me to come nigh,
To see You as You are, I must look inward
And have my eyes anointed from on high.

For fragrant airs of heaven do surround You,
And when the veil is taken from my sight,
I see You as You truly are, all glorious,
Surrounded, bathed, immersed in heaven's light.

Your sorrows are transformed into such beauty
I cannot bear to turn away my gaze,
I see made real the names the Father gave You,
And bow in worship, adoration, praise.

How beautiful You are, O my Redeemer,
King of Glory, spotless Lamb You are,
The Rose of Sharon, Lily of the Valley,
The Light of Heaven and the Morning Star.

One thing
I ask of the Lord . . .
to gaze upon
the beauty of the Lord
and to seek Him
in His temple.
Psalm 27:4 NIV

The Country of Gethsemane

A burnt out land

The tree stumps charred
And smoke filled sky
No bird song in the air
Nor green to meet the eye

A thunder roll
A lightning flash
Yet look – ahead I see
His footprints in the ash

Even though I walk
through the valley
of the shadow of death,
I will fear no evil,
for You
are
with me.
Psalm 23:4 NIV

Deadly Poison

Envenomed blade
Slips in and out
Swift fatal thrust
Like snickersnee
And leaves no mark

Yet deep within
The victim bleeds
And dies a silent death

Encarmined tongue
How can you walk away
Unscathed?

No man
can
tame
the tongue.
It is
a restless
evil,
full of
deadly
poison.
James 3:8 NIV

The Pool of Years

The pure sweet drops fall gently to
Our stretched out hands with which we take
This gift, each drop a year from Him

And as we cup our earthstained hands
And vainly try to stem the flow
We see our seasons come and go

Remorseless march the drops of time
The steady passing of our days
Into the pool of gathering years

Our hands have stained this gift of His
And so we see our darksome pond
All mud and mire from our own earth

But then we see the pool transformed
For there He stands with bloodstained hands
To cleanse it, so that gazing in

He sees His face reflected there
In waters still and crystalline
And by its edge His garden grows

My
times
are
in
Your
hands.
Psalm 31:15 NIV

Sorrow and Jubilee

I, Mary
Stood at the foot of the cross
And watched You die, Lord
Watched Death reach out to take You where I cannot go
Watched the end of everything

For I loved You, Lord
Loved You because you saw
through the hardness and filth of my life
And knew that I was weeping inwardly
Knew my desolation and despair
And reached out and drew me to You
And forgave it all and made me clean again
Gave me life and hope and joy

And now, Lord, Your life is gone
And I feel the anguish and the grief
And Death has taken You away
And now what shall we do?
For all is over and our lives are ended too
And we'll go home again and You're not there

You drew me out to love You, Lord
And now You're gone and I feel more lonely than before
And I weep sadly through the night
And would not see tomorrow
But it comes
And with it all the endless days ahead
Without You near to make my life worthwhile

Let me die too for there is nothing now
And I shake my fist but it's no use
And I sink into despair

And then the morning came
A dark and gloomy dawn
I would not understand nor wish to see
If there were brightness after yesterday
How would the dewdrops dare to glisten
Or birds break forth in song?

So I, Mary
Went to Your grave to weep
And to be with You while I could
But found You not!

Instead the stone was gone and two white angels
Sat within to ask me why I wept
Blinded by my tears I saw a man
And asked where You had gone

And then You said my name!
Not know that Voice?
My name so often spoken
In derision by young lads
Contempt by wives and mothers
With curses and with scorn by rough hewn men

Only You had said it with that accent of pure love
And suddenly I knew
That only God can say
"I have called you by your name and Mine you are."

And so I knew, did not need to touch,
That Voice alone enough to know You lived!
Death's spectre vanished and now the sun could shine
Your Resurrection Day
And, as it were, a second one for me

Weeping may tarry for the night,
but joy comes with the morning. Psalm 30:5 RSV

Biography

Just a dog-eared ordinary notebook
Thumbed over, underlined,
A corner of a page turned down,
Some ink blots here and there
(That stain, I think, was lunch!)
Some sheets are pulling loose
And I can't even find
Page twenty-seven.

Can You, oh God,
Take and write on this,
The pages of my life,
Correct and edit
This manuscript
With bold and flowing strokes
And make a tale worth reading?

Then I said,
"Lo, I come;
in the roll
of the book
it is written
of me."
Psalm 40:7 RSV

Growing Up

O see him there, the chestnut foal,
He scampers on the grass,
Untamed and lively does He go,
His hoofbeats gaily pass,
The meadow wide his happy home,
The universe his air,
Nor God nor man does slow him down,
He lives without a care.

Then comes the day when he is caught
And put within a fence,
He struggles, understands it not,
For nothing can he sense
Of why his freedom should be lost,
His days of play be done,
Why he must stay within these walls
And not be free to run.

And then he sees the form of one
Who stands there by the gate,
His owner, who had been for years
Content to stand and wait.
But now with bridle in his hand
He moves to tame his own
And bring him to the place where he
Can deal with him alone.

His shaggy, dull and mottled coat
Is brushed and made to glow,
And gentle hands reach out to give
Him food with which to grow.
A quiet voice begins to speak
And bids his fears depart,
And slowly fans a flame of love
Within that restless heart.

And as that flame becomes a blaze
He finds there is a key,
And giving up his own self-will
Has made him truly free.
O see him now, full grown, mature,
His passions now are stilled,
And disciplined by love he finds
His own desires fulfilled.

Be not
like a horse
or a mule,
without understanding,
which must
be curbed
with bit
and bridle,
else it will
not keep
with you.
Psalm 32:9 RSV

Antarctica

Across an arctic frozen plain
The silence reigns
The frigid wastes permit no sound
Not even ice floes creaking in the sea

And if a voice should speak
'Twould be as one who tolls a bell
In some far off church tower
And in the congealed icy air
The sound would carry free for miles
Though distant, faint but clear

Yet all is still

And if I speak
It is as if a small round stone
Fell from flaccid hand into the sea
So smooth there is no splash
Nor ripple to disturb

So finally I'm mute

And so it is when God is still
And friends are gone
Have stopped their ears or think they know
And I am dumb

How can love or friendship grow
In such a place as this?

Oh God and friends
Berate me if you will
Rebuke with dark, with flame, with pain
But oh do not be silent!

To You I call,
O Lord my rock;
For if you remain silent,
I will be
like those
who have gone down
to the pit.
Psalm 28:1 NIV

Sowing in Tears

He wept
    and stored his tears within a clear and crystal flask
    that sparkled in the sun
    so he could see the level rise
    and yet it never filled
    for unbeknownst to him an inner flaw
    had let the tears escape
    to make a muddy slough around his feet
    because they were self-pity

He wept
    this time the Lord brought forth a precious lovely vase
    of gold and silver made
    fit for the temple service
    in which to keep the tears
    for these were those which are to all men given
    who walk the earth
    designed to bring them near to His own side
    for they are pain and sorrow

He wept
    a row of marred and battered broken earthen pots
    were set before him now
    and as the jars were filled
    God counted every tear
    and carried them away to His own secret place
    far from the eyes of men
    only vessels such as these could hold the pure
    and holy tears of intercession

You have collected
all my tears
and preserved them
in your bottle.
Psalm 56:8 TLB

Tempest

It's just a little boat
Out in the deep
Surrounded by the mountains of the sea
And shore is out of sight

The sides are high and steep
Protecting from the crests
The boat His hand
Cupped to hold me safe

He reaches down to plant
A mast and little sail
Faith to catch the wind
And send me on my way

And when a storm descends
And fear has grabbed the helm
He simply lifts His hand
A while till stillness comes

He
stilled the storm
to a whisper.
. . .
They were glad
when it grew calm
and He guided them
to their desired haven.
Psalm 107:29-30 NIV

The Peaceable Kingdom

From secret springs and freshets clear,
From high in meadows fair,
Through mountain passes deep and cool,
Through sunlit, sparkling air,
Through darkest nights and radiant days
The waters ever flow,
Refreshing all they touch upon
As seasons come and go.

This river is God's mercy, grace,
His wisdom, peace, and love,
His joy and blessed quietness
All flowing from above.

It dashes down the steeper slopes
Adorned with mist and spray,
A rainbow shimmers as it falls
To make its rockstrewn way.
It winds through placid, level lands,
Its waters deep and slow,
It captures stars on moonlit nights,
By day sun's burnished glow.

The land through which this river flows,
Its name is Paradise,
And only those can enter in
Who see with children's eyes.

Upon its banks the lions play
With fawn, gazelle, and doe,
The tigers romp with elephants,
And mice with kittens grow,
The leopard watches without lust
The new foal and its dam,

For nature is at peace within
The Kingdom of the Lamb.

All golden in the sun and shade,
The flowers on the rim
Lift up their faces to the sun
And so rejoice in Him.

The fruited trees on either side,
The vineyards in the sun,
My food provide from day to day,
Where'er the waters run.
I cup my hands, refreshing draughts
Are mine to take at will,
And though my thirst may be profound,
I always have my fill.

To be a child in Paradise,
How wonderful to be
Unchained from self and all its cares,
To truly be set free.

I skip beside the living stream,
By shadowed pools I lie,
I wade in shallows, swim in depths,
And contemplate the sky.
I stand beneath the waterfall,
I bathe and splash and sing,
I wash my head, my hands, my feet,
Refreshing does it bring.

Thy river of delights, O Lord,
Thy land most passing fair,
I pray for grace to enter in
And dwell forever there.

Thou
givest
them drink
from
the river
of Thy delights.
Psalm 36:8 RSV

Courage

The way was steep
And choked with weeds and briars
And fears that I had sown so long ago
Were now so high
There was no way
That I could pass

When suddenly
He came!

And walking by my side
He trod them down
And others in full bloom
He just reached down
And plucked them out
And tossed them to the side

The way still steep
And dusty, strewn with stones,
But found I now
I could go on

The angel of the Lord
encamps
around
those
who fear Him,
and He
delivers them.
Psalm 34:7 NIV

Unseen Presence

It's very dark
    Is that You I see standing there
    A lantern in Your hand?

It's very still
    Is that so that the only voice
    That I can hear is Yours?

It seems so cold
    Is that a fire You've lit ahead
    Where I can warm my heart?

I feel alone
    Is that Your step I hear behind
    Upon the dusty trail?

The way seems steep
    Is it Your hand that's reaching down
    To help me up the cliff?

In all the darknesses of life
You always have been there

Even the darkness
will
not be dark
to You.
Psalm 139:12 NIV

Wedding Day

Tall, lithe and beautiful He stood
the patient bridegroom in His glowing robes
and thought about His bride
Before Him spread on tables lay the cloth
a wealth of living glowing flame
fine damask, wool, and cool crisp linen
And royal hands reached in to sift and sort
among the pulsing vivid glow
to find a proper garment for His bride
And to one side there lay a smaller pile
of jewels, rich warm and deep in hue
reflecting prisms of the sun
"How beautiful she'll be," He said,
"this color for her eyes, dove's eyes,
and this will match her hair."

And there she stood when brought before the throne
in meager ragged frock with dirty face
and shivering from her fear
And wondered at the summons to the King
for well she knew her sorry state
(is this what He has deigned to call His own?)
For what she felt within was shame
to stand before Him in her rags
and so she hid her face from that clear gaze
Little did she know He saw her not
as she appeared without but was within
for looked He at the inner chambers of Her heart
To see if they would match His own
and when He saw that inner flame
He cried with joy, "She is for me!"

So then He washed her face and bathed her
  in the aromatic ointments of the East
  and with great care He dressed her
Himself prepared her for the wedding
  and over all a cloak of feathers
  His hedge around her of protection
And all the garments fit as He had chosen
  because they were the true
  adornings of her heart
Transformed she was when taken to His side
  two hearts rejoicing in each other
  in deep fulfilled and consummated love
She was as a whole company of those
  whose heartbeat is as one
  with Him and with each other.

The king
will
desire
your
beauty.
Since He is
your lord,
bow to Him.
Psalm 45:11 RSV

Longings

O still-born words and feeble tongue!
O eyes that cannot see!
In silent anguish yearns my soul
To follow after Thee.

I would see Thee and Thee alone
Yet veils obscure my eyes,
The darkness of my inner sin
Has brought me cloudy skies.

I with this voice would tell Thee much,
And yet I am struck dumb,
In silence do I long for Thee
With words that will not come.

How pitiful my earthbound clay!
How heavy is its chain!
How strong the power that would me keep
From what I would attain.

Yet somehow through the fog and mist
My spirit can leap free
And flee straight to Thy loving heart
That longs indeed for me.

And so my thirsty soul can drink
While cradled on Thy breast,
And understanding needs no words
To bring me into rest.

Yet long I for the day to come
When veils will not be seen,
And I behold Thee face to face
With nothing in-between.

And then, behold, my song shall rise,
My lips indeed be free,
For all my self will then be gone
And lost indeed in Thee.

And then my rest, O dearest Lord,
Will blessed come to be
Complete and perfect in Thy arms
As I am one with Thee.

For
God
alone
my soul
waits
in silence.
Psalm 62:1 RSV

Idols

Man upon the throne
Within my soul?
How could it be?
For long ago I'd made a vow
That He be first
Yet deep within I'd known
It was not so

For I took my cares
And heedless ran
To scatter them
And worship at the thrones of men
In hopes that they
Would understand and free
Me from my pain

Rushing to and fro
I lost the path
And left Him to
One side for other's words and ways
And nigh drowned out
That one clear Voice within
Amidst the throng

Then, when made aware
And conscious of
The feet of clay
Of gods and my unfaithful heart
I gathered up
The fragments and then knelt
Before His throne

Jealous God of mine
Who loves to draw
And separate
Take this divided heart and make
It one and grant
A single eye to dwell
On You alone

Give me
an undivided heart,
that I may
fear Your Name.
Psalm 86:11 NIV

His Path

Step carefully — the path is laid just so
That in His way your footsteps safely go
From stone to stone, the order long since planned,
To bring you on into His promised land.

Walk softly — for the holy way you tread
Was walked by Him whose very blood was shed
To make a way for weary pilgrim feet
That search to find a rest that is complete.

Kneel down — for when you reach a certain height
The way is steep, though bathed in His own light,
And only on your knees can you progress,
Or even dare approach His holiness.

Be still — you walk in company with One
Who knew the worlds before they were begun,
Yet stooped to take your hands within His own,
To bring you ever closer to His throne.

Look up — and keep your gaze upon His face,
And do not step beyond His given grace,
The way is long, the dangers real and grim,
Your only sure defense to stay with Him.

Then hark — for midst the clamor of life's day
There is the Voice of Jesus to obey,
Your ears must be attuned to hear His call,
To keep you safe and guard you from a fall.

Stretch out — your hand and take His very own,
You cannot tread this weary path alone,
One Guide and One alone as nears the end,
Your dear Companion and your blessed Friend.

Look back — but only when the journey's past,
And you have reached God's place for you at last,
Then with your lips speak out and humbly say,
"It was His grace– He led me all the way."

In all your ways
acknowledge
Him
and He
will
make
your
paths
straight.
Proverbs 3:6 NIV

Refiner

Among the things
That man demands
Is precious gold
Within his hands

Gold hard and strong
So he can take
And from his hoard
An idol make

Alloyed, impure
It stands alone
And man kneels down
Before its throne

Its brassy glare
Attracts his eyes
And worshipping
Its form he dies

But with great care
Our God refines
And purifies
The gold He mines

He wants it soft
Within His hand
To move and flow
At His command

Only when pure
Can He then mold
His own desire
From pliant gold

Alive, aglow
Its burnished skin
Reflects the life
That dwells within

When He
has tested me,
I will come forth
as gold.
Job 23:10 NIV

Seasons

Hold out your hands
For when He gives, He giveth much,
No partial drops or passing shower
But with abundant love and grace
For no good gift does He withhold

Hold out your hands
For even when the drought lies hard
Upon the land, a work is done,
For only thirsty ones can drink
When falls the rain that comes from God

Hold out your hands
For He has more in store for you
To bring that land to bear its fruit
His plow and harrow work must do
As seasons come and seasons go

Hold out your hands
And bless the sunshine or the rains
Or snow, or winds, or heat, or chill,
Receiving all with grateful heart
His gifts will do the needed work

For everything
there is
a season,
and a time
for every matter
under heaven.
Ecclesiastes 3:1 RSV

Voice from the Dust

I am as cardboard
Thin flat and gray
Once I had a life of three dimensions
Had form and shape and space within
But now God's hand is heavy laid
And pressed me down He has
For His eternal purposes and plan
And even yet
I cannot cry to be redeemed

Brought low,
you will
speak from the ground;
your speech
will mumble
out of the dust.
Your voice
will come
ghostlike
from the earth;
. . .
suddenly,
in an instant,
the Lord Almighty
will come.
Isaiah 29:4–6 NIV

Arrogance

O heart
that stands on two strong legs before the throne
and dares to look the Father in the eye
explain your case
defend your way
and stand there in your pride

O heart
search for humility and wrap its cloak
close tight around you and then hide your face
Ask to be shown
your willful state
and prostrate fall in shame

O heart
retreat in awe until He bids you stand
nor dare to lift your eyes above the ground
in silence deep
with thy lips closed
and wait for Him to speak

How long
will you refuse
to humble yourself
before Me?
Exodus 10:3 NIV

Shulamite

Who is this from the wilderness now coming,
Who leans on her Beloved's strong right arm?
The ashes from her past still lie upon her
For leaping hungry fires have done her harm.

From whence she comes is veiled and deeply shadowed,
A wilderness where wild beasts roam at will,
It is the land called Desolate, Forsaken,
A place that leaves its mark upon her still.

Her Lover has come down to draw her to Him,
The flame of great desire within His eyes,
He sees her, not as black, but very comely,
His fair one, if she could but realize.

With sad and wondering eyes she turned to see Him,
For shamed, she had withdrawn to hide her face,
She meant that neither God nor man should find her,
And chose to be alone in her disgrace.

A gray and mourning dove she had retreated,
The cleft within the rock would hide her nest,
But winter's chilly fingers had betrayed her,
For icy rains and snow gave her no rest.

For men had made her tend their many vineyards,
Alas, her very own she could not keep,
She felt the sun scorch both her and the harvest,
And so, dismayed, could only stop and weep.

He kissed her, set His seal upon her, loved her,
Spoke tenderly and called her "O my dove,"
He brought her to His banquet house of cedar,
His banner over her, undying Love.

Instead of shame, her portion shall be double,
Instead of ashes, garlands for her head,
The oil of gladness shall replace the mourning,
And confidence shall take away her dread.

The land to which she comes is full of blossoms,
The fragrance of the fig trees fills the air,
The turtledoves rejoice in radiant sunshine,
And spring has made the landscape pure and fair.

Her King has chosen her as His companion,
His pleasure is to have her by His side,
And as He purifies and so transforms her,
He knows that one day she will be His Bride.

My dove
in the clefts
of the rock
. . .
show me
your face,
let me
hear
your voice.
Song of Solomon 2:14 NIV

Night Hours

In the still night hours
When all around me is placid and at rest
And my body still listens to the day's demands
And the hours pass quietly one by one toward the dawn
Then the only rest I know, the only rest I find
Is in You, Lord

You reach down Your gentle hand and touch my brow
And when You say "Peace, be still"
My body cannot seem to hear
But my spirit sighs and says "Yes Lord"
And the assent brings quietness
And I know You are here
And I lean my head upon Your hand

Talk to me, Lord
In these fragile hours that soon will disappear
Come and talk to me
As two lovers spend the night careless of their sleep
Their conversation too precious for slumber to cut off

Let me delight in Your presence, Lord,
Let me hear Your Voice
And tell me what I need to know

And instead of my noisy clamor ringing in Your ears
Tell me what is in Your heart
And what You want to say

Upon my bed at night,
I sought Him whom my soul loves
. . .
I held Him and would not let Him go.
Song of Solomon 3:1,4 RSV

Self Condemnation

To stand there for my trial
    With hands before me tied
And know that all the universe
    In speaking of me lied

How strange it seemed to be
    Beneath that brazen sky
Judge, jury, executioner
    All were I.

There
is
only
one
Lawgiver
and
Judge.
James 4:12 NIV

Nocturnal Garden

My room will be a garden, Lord,
And the night hours
The time the Gardener walks alone
And bends over His flowers
And cares for them
And the gentle rain of His love
Soaks into the earth
And where the pruning has been done
New buds and life spring forth

Awake,
north wind,
and come,
south wind!
Blow
on my garden,
that its fragrance
may spread
abroad.
Song of Solomon 4:16 NIV

Into His Hands

Just touch me with Your hands, O Lord,
No others can I bear,
The wounds are grievous and so deep
They need the Shepherd's care.

O lift me with Your gentle touch,
And hold me to Your breast,
And then, O touch my fevered heart
And bring me into rest.

I trust myself to You alone,
To You in love I press,
You know the ills of mind and soul,
You see my deep distress.

Your hands have touched the lepers' sores,
Have opened blind men's eyes,
Caressed the heads of little ones,
And made a lame man rise.

Your blessed hands will help me too,
Will ease me with their touch,
For sure am I that in Your ears
My cry availeth much.

I look and see upon Your palms
My name engraven there,
And so I know beyond all doubt
You will my anguish bear.

The imprint of those two great nails
Remains so plain to see,
You know my inner pain because
You felt that agony.

Your hands do tell me that You are
The Refuge of the weak,
The Shepherd of the weary flock,
The Hope of all the meek.

And so with faith and trust I leave
My wounded spirit there,
Within the safety of Your hands,
Within my Shepherd's care.

See,
I have
engraved you
on
the palms
of
My hands.
Isaiah 49:16 NIV

Broken Cisterns

How sad
    To reach down in my well
    Expect a bucket brimming
    To find that its gone dry
    And know I cannot meet
    Another's need

But sadder yet
    To find the cistern full
    With water that's not living
    And slake another's thirst
    From my own stagnant well
    And never know

They . . .
have dug
their own
cisterns,
broken
cisterns
that
cannot
hold
water.
Jeremiah 2:13 NIV

New Life

The Great and Morning Star reached out
And plucked a tiny star from His own universe
And sent her down to you – His child, not yours –
A piece of heaven still in her fragile hand
And in her eyes, still focused on His face,
That light which speaks of heaven's realms

We look upon this child and see the mystery
Of new and precious life – conceived and wrought
In His own heart and mind from time long past –
Created by His gentle hands – a work in miniature –
So intricate and finely formed – so delicate
The detailed beauty of her frame

And so He gives this perfect gift to you
And through her coming to your lives
May there be wrought within that perfect work
Of which she is a sign – an inner precious thing –
Shaped by those hands whose firm and gentle touch
Creates a spirit that is pleasing in His sight

Before I
formed you
in the womb
I knew you,
before you
were born
I set you
apart.
Jeremiah 1:5 NIV

Solitary Saints

Invisible!
Wrong kind of transparency
Yet solid made
Of flesh and blood and bone and brain
They pass along the earth
More silent than a wraith
Walk through snow
And leave no print
Speak with words unheard
Unseen by all but few

What mean such separated lives
That no one sees or hears?
For whom and why do they exist?
What coinage are they worth?

Cloistered by His hand
Unknown, despised
Forgotten or ignored
They seem so rare
Their value must be high
And measured in a currency
That we know nothing of

God's silent solitary ones

I
sat
alone
because
Your hand
was
on me.
Jeremiah 15:17 NIV

Reluctance

Clay! I'm just clay?
  I don't like the sound of that!
  It's only common mud, You know
  So surely You are joking!

And then let someone else's hands
  Take and shape the vessel
  of the only life I have?
  No thank you, Lord!

Somehow I'd rather reach down deep
  Within myself with my own hands
  And make a shape I'd like to be
  And have it my own choice

And fire it in some gentle flame
  Not those fearsome kilns of Yours
  I see those people here and there
  And wonder how they stood the fire

And yet

  It's just that deep within I know
  There is no other way to go
  Pots made by novices and cheap
  Must make the Master Potter weep

But the pot he was shaping . . .
was marred . . .
so the potter formed it
into another pot,
shaping it as seemed best to him.
Jeremiah 18:4 NIV

Birdlover

With feathers so battered and torn from the fight
The little bird flutters to rest from its plight,
Wounded its heart and forlorn its weak cry,
It is far from its nest and unable to fly.

Gently the Master stoops down in pure love,
Cradles the hurt one and brings it above,
Holding it tenderly close to His breast,
He wants it to find there peace and sweet rest.

O little bird, cease your struggles and lie
Safe in His hands with the Comforter nigh,
The oil of forgiveness He pours on your head,
And pardon's complete as the Savior has said.

The wounds of the battle will heal in His care,
And then He will toss you back in the air,
Free to fly onward and up with a song,
Knowing that guilt and all fear now have gone.

For I
will restore
health
to you,
and your wounds
I will heal,
says the Lord.
Jeremiah 30:17 RSV

The Net Maker

With patient skill His fingers wove the net
Of gossamer, the knots so tight, and yet
Strong and fragile, as Love itself can be,
The weave so fine that scarcely eye could see

And with great care He cast it out to fall
As soft and gentle as the Spirit's call
Light as a sigh or whisper on the air
It tangled with the figure standing there

Then gently drew He in the folds so tight
And drew the burden up into the light,
And bound to Him by silken cords of love
I was set free to live His life above

I
have loved you
with
an everlasting
love;
I
have drawn you
with
loving-kindness.
Jeremiah 31:3 NIV

Storms

Raindrops His tears
Thunder His voice
Wind His joy
Lightning His gaze
Clouds His peace
Darkness His love
Hail His might
Snow His balm

Waiting and then

Rainbow His vow

Only storms
Make rainbows

I have set
My rainbow
in the clouds.
Genesis 9:13 NIV

Contrasts

Desolation
a gray forbidding isle that looms
from out a dark and angry sea
assaulted by fierce winds and gales
devoid of life its barren shores
Consolation
one's little boat hard driven past
and carried to the other side
to find calm sunny harbor there
protected from the wildest storms

Desolation
a lonely rock in desert sands
which bakes in blazing heat of day
and cracks in frigid nighttime air
and shudders as the wind whips past
Consolation
the shadow cast on sunless side
to shade the weary traveler
and tiny hidden secret pools
left there by early morning dew

Desolation
a stark white berg in arctic seas
a beautiful but frozen mass
its aimless path and hidden bulk
a secret menace in the sea
Consolation
the unseen winds and currents strong
that steer it on its southward way
where slowly it begins to melt
in warmer climes and sunnier days

Desolation
　　a sheer and towering granite cliff
　　whose ascent must be made alone
　　no way the eye can trace a path
　　nor ropes nor guides to reach the goal
Consolation
　　to reach a straining groping hand
　　for one small hold in creviced wall
　　and find a small but lovely flower
　　unseen by all but him who climbs

Desolation
　　a walk among a silent throng
　　tight wrapped in cloaks with faces veiled
　　and be unable to reach out
　　and speak a word or ask for bread
Consolation
　　to sudden see amidst the crowd
　　a long and well remembered face
　　your Friend stood long to see you pass
　　and give a warm and sure embrace

Are
the consolations
of God
too small
for you?
Job 15:11 RSV

The Great Physician

With surgeon's skill His gentle fingers
Reached into one poor frayed and tattered
Human heart
And gently separated out the strands –
Each bruised and battered filament
Repaired, made whole, its damage healed –
Some strands so willingly came forth
But others painfully and slow
As they could bear the separation
From earth's tenacious grasp

And then He slowly knit and wove them
One by one, each in its time –
According to its destiny, capacity,
Into the glowing fabric of that great heart of His –
Each strand so intimately linked and intertwined
That when His heart beat, so did the other –
Experienced each sorrow, longing, joy and pain
Of His – identified in purpose and intent –
Two made one– a mystery that only comes about
When we are one with Him

I
will give you
a new heart
and put
a new spirit
in you.
Ezekiel 36:26 NIV

Dim Vision

Bright shining trusting eyes of little folk
Awaiting each new day
Believing in the goodness and the love
Of those who care for them

Bright shining trusting eyes of faithful pets
Who trust their owners' love
Believing in the hand that gives them food
And gives them love's caress

Why is it only I, so "wise, mature,"
Not trusting in my Lord
Who face the future trembling and afraid
With eyes obscured by doubt?

Jesus . . .
reached out
His hand
. . .
saying, to him,,
'O man
of little faith,
why
did
you
doubt?'
Matthew 14:31 RSV

Exchange

Upon the tree Your anguished form
Was stretched in agony for me
And as I see Your body torn
I am brought to humility.

I lift my gaze to see Your face,
Those clear and penetrating eyes
Look deep within to give me grace
And let me know that I shall rise

Someday from off this cross of mine,
And which to Thine has no compare,
But sent to me with love divine
To teach me how Thy death to share.

O Lord, my cross that bends me low
Is just Your grace to bring me to
The place to let my own life go
And find instead new life in You.

O give me grace to find it light,
To feel the joy You want to give,
Upon Your cross to set my sight,
And lose my life that I might live.

Whoever finds
his life
will lose it,
and whoever
loses
his life
for My sake
will find it.
Matthew 10:39 NIV

Portrait

He walks before me –
His bare feet stir the dust of Palestine
He takes the paths the Father does ordain
And reckons not the cost in grief or pain
And tells His Lord "Thy will is ever Mine"
And I must follow.

He walks before me –
The light of heaven dwells upon His face,
His eyes are set on unseen things above,
Yet turned to man in pity and in love,
And from His inner being flows sweet grace
And I must follow.

He walks before me –
His robe that of a lowly man and meek,
With nought to show He is the King on high,
Wrapped in humility He comes to die,
No crown, no throne, no glory does He seek,
And I must follow.

He walks before me –
He stumbles as He climbs up Calvary's hill,
And needs a hand to help Him on the way,
Embraces shame and death as if to say,
"My only joy is in My Father's will"
And I must follow.

He walks before me
This humble, lowly, sacrificial Lamb
Is lifted up before my wondering eyes,
The burden of my sin upon Him lies,
To bring to death the very Son of Man,
And I must follow.

He walks before me –
    My eyes so filled with tears can barely see,
    With hands outstretched there stands the Crucified,
    The wounds still bleeding from His hands, His side,
    In anguish and in love He calls to me,
And I must follow.

He
who
does not
take his cross
and
follow Me
is not
worthy
of Me.
Matthew 10:38 RSV

Platitude

To speak and say I love His will
Is easy work at best,
The words flow smoothly from my tongue
When never put to test

But oh, the stark reality
Is something else instead,
And find I that this discipline
Is harder lived than said.

This people
honors Me
with their lips
but their heart
is
far
from Me.
Mark 7:6 RSV

Petition

As I cling to the hem of His garment,
And kneel at my dear Saviour's feet,
There still rises within me a longing,
A sense that I am not complete.

For I long to be raised to His bosom,
His arms to encircle me there,
And to give myself over completely,
A little child kept in His care.

Not stay down at His feet ever seeking,
But lying there close to His breast,
To be one of His lambs, oh so needy,
That finds there its comfort and rest.

For a look in His eyes will suffice me,
To know I am one with Him there,
And I'll know I have left all behind me
To trust myself into His care.

So I ask Thee, dear Jesus, to lift me,
To bring me so close to Thy heart,
That my life is just lost in Thy being,
No more from Thee ever to part.

To be lost in Thy love, oh how glorious,
To live and to breathe only Thee,
For to know I am one with Thee, Jesus,
Can only be heaven for me.

Simon Peter said to him,
'Lord, not my feet only
but also my hands and my head!'
John 13:9 RSV

Bittersweet

His hands hold out this cup to me
To drink, blessed, heavenly hands,
So scarred and torn by cruel nails
And bleeding still, from wounds
Of men (and me), who bring fresh
Daily sorrow to His heart.

Those anguished, loving eyes
Look into mine and ask if
I will drink of what He has
Prepared for me. Can bleak
Gethsemane be shared?
And will I die as crucified?

His blessed Voice speaks that the draught
Is made especially for me:
"Look not on others' portions, but
Thine own. Just this is now
Prepared for you, made in heaven
For your good. Oh, drink of Me."

And as those hands lift to my lips
The bitter draught, then flinch I would
And tarry, push it from me
But when I see that what I
Yearned for all my life is not to be
So He can give me something better,

Then to my lips, oh press the cup,
And let me drink it to
The very dregs. And as I taste,
How strangely sweet the bitter grows
As I accept His sovereign way
And die the death He wills.

Are
you
able
to
drink
the cup?
Matthew 20:22 RSV

Growing Season

The springtime rains have soaked my earth
And now I wait to see new birth
O may I reach whate'er condition
Will bring my life to full fruition

My Lord has touched my life and so
Through Him alone the fruits will grow
O give me grace to onward press
And come into His righteousness

He will give
the rain for your land
in its season,
the early rain
and the later rain,
that you may gather in
your grain
and your wine
and your oil.
Deuteronomy 11:14 RSV

Waverings

If I give You all my being
Will You take away my freedom?
Will You bring me into bondage?
Will You make the way seem hard?
O My child of little courage
I will give you life fulfilling,
I will break the chains that bind you,
I will flood your path with mercy,
I will give you all of Me.

If I give You all my burdens
Can I trust You not to drop them,?
Can I cease the endless effort?
Can I leave them all to You?
O My child, so overburdened
I would carry them so safely,
I would free your mind from fretting,
I would lift the load so heavy,
You can trust them all to Me.

If I let down my defenses
Should I unprotected be?
Should I find the fight o'erwhelming?
Should I fail my quest for Thee?
O My child, with faith so feeble
Take My sword to fight the battle,
Take My armor to protect you,
Hide your life in My protection,
Wars are never lost with Me.

If I lose my life in serving
Will its loss too costly be?
Will the pain involved in dying
Prove to be too much for me?
O My child, with fears so mighty
Find your rest and peace in Me,
Know that dying is just passing
Into new life, pure and free.
Come and live that life with Me.

Let us hold
unswervingly
to the hope
we profess,
for He who promised
is
faithful.
Hebrews 10:23 NIV

The Fall

"Lord,
my clasp on You
is so tight
I will never let You go
nor leave Your side"
so I swore
in my innocence

until that day came
when my fingers loosened
and how I fell
when the shaking came
and all my
vows so swiftly
came to nought

my strength gone
like a feeble promise
lost in the emptiness
of voids around me
the words unheard
the resolve undone

for all I longed for
I could not hold
and so the swift
descent
through misted worlds
of empty self
to bleak despairs

but in the midst
of the swooning fall
His hand reached down
and caught me there
suspended
between the futile
efforts of my soul
and the bedrock
of His
certainties

sinewy fingers
with gentle touch
held me tight
yet bruised me not
and set me
once again
on the sure foundation
of His being
my tight clenched
foolish hands
so hard had striven
to keep Him close
mortality
thinking it could hold
divinity
when just the opposite
is true

Let any one
who thinks
that he stands
take heed
lest he fall.
1 Corinthians 10:12 RSV

The Prison of His Will

I fought and wrestled with my chains
Of circumstance, Another's will,
Unable to accept their weight,
Unable to find rest, be still.
Impenetrable prison walls
Reduced me had to deep despair,
I knew that hope forever gone
Of breathing freedom's scented air.

But when to quietness I came
And looked up from my agony,
I saw the chains were beaten gold,
Quite fragile and of filigree,
With script that only I could read,
The letters saying "Peace, be still"
I saw the links were Perfect Love,
Compassion, and His Blessed Will.

My eyes to that barred window strayed
And saw a lark go soaring by,
Its sweet cadenza brought my soul
And spirit to another sky,
And through that opening high above
The sunshine poured to touch my head,
And on the fragrant breeze there blew
The whispered words which He had said.

And then the walls began to gleam
In iridescent shades and hue,
They looked like shimmering curtains which
I saw I freely could pass through,
Transformed my cell to Paradise,
A place of beauty all aglow,
And joy began to lift my head
Although I could not come and go.

For though I may leave if I choose,
I find my will Another's now,
Extend my hands for Him to take,
Although I know not where nor how.
The fetters are His cords of love,
And so I find captivity
Will bring me rest and quietness
And in His arms I shall be free.

Where
the Spirit
of
the Lord
is,
there is
freedom.
2 Corinthians 3:17 RSV

Master Tailor

Experienced fingers laid the pattern on the cloth
And then began to cut
To make the unformed cloth into the shape he needed –
A tailor busy at his work

Does cloth feel pain as scissors bite its strands?
I know I do
When master shears are trimming off the excess of my life
And "Stop" is what I want to shriek

Until I hear a voice that says
"No, wait, I know what I'm about –
This is the only pattern that will fit
The shape and contours of your life –

And do not fret –
I've made a lot of suits!"

For
we
are
God's
work-
man-
ship.
Ephesians 2:10 NIV

Two Crosses

Reach down from Your cross
O Son of Man
And lift me up to mine
Take those rough hewn nails
And cleave me to Your blessed will
And if I struggle
Heed me not
Enough to know
You hang beside me

I
have
been
crucified
with
Christ.
Galatians 2:20 NIV

Maturity

As Mary once
Did nurse within
That precious spark
Of Jesus' life
To let Him grow
Begin to move
Come forth one day
In perfect form
Restrained a while
Until the day
She set Him free
To destiny
When He had reached
Maturity

So nurse I too
His life within
A seed that I
Let live or die
Can let Him grow
Or stifle Him
Can set Him free
To work within
Till He come forth
As He desires
And live His life
Instead of mine
When I have reached
Maturity

Christ
in you,
the hope
of glory.
Colossians 1:27 NIV

King of Kings

"King" they hailed, and laughed as they beheld Him,
Clad with royal purple and with thorn,
"King" they jeered and mocked as they provoked Him,
Cursed the day on which He had been born,
"King" they wrote in blood and nailed it o'er Him,
As they hung Him on His cross of shame,
"King" they cried, but bound and smote and scourged Him,
Jesting as they spoke that sacred Name.

"King" said Pilate, Jesus there before him,
Washed his hands and fed Him to the crowd,
"King" had Peter said before he failed Him,
Though in earnest he had firmly vowed,
"King" disciples said, while some in secret
Hoped to be the ones at His right hand,
"King" cried many as they waved their branches,
Shouting what they did not understand.

Few there were who understood His coming,
Few who let Him reign upon His throne,
Few who bowed their knees and hearts in earnest,
Saw Him as their Sovereign King alone,
Few there were who pledged themselves as bondslaves,
Ready to obey, cost what it would,
Few who knew this carpenter was royal,
Gave to Him all that they were and could.

Am I in that throng that so betrays Him,
Even though disciple I might be?
Am I one whose lips so quickly praise Him,
But do not achieve humility?
Do I call Him King and not obey Him,
Should my path through difficulty lie?
Can I kneel and tell Him I adore Him,
When He tells me just how I must die?

Oh, to make Him King would truly please Him,
Comfort Him, assuage His wounded heart,
How He would rejoice to have me crown Him,
Make Him King of all, not just a part,
Make of me a slave to freely serve Him,
Finding all my joy in Him alone,
Knowing that to be in bondage to Him,
Frees me to become His very own.

The blessed
and
only
Sovereign,
the King
of kings
and
Lord
of lords
. . .
To Him
be
honor
and
eternal
dominion.
1 Timothy 6:15-16 RSV

Holocaust

He let His life be
Immolated
Consumed on the altar
By pure bright flame
Freely He suffered
And was reduced to ashes
From which there sprang
That Rose of Sharon
Beautiful in morning dew
And fragrant on the air

So too, dear Lord,
Burn my earth and dust
With Thy molten fire
Regardless of the pain
Reduce me to my nothingness
A suffering less than Thine
But gladly given
From which I may exchange
My ashes for Thy beauty
My earthly life for Thine

For
our God
is
a
consuming
fire.
Hebrews 12:29 NIV

The Inner Life

O my soul
Like Isaac be
In his great
Humility
Bound there by
His father's will
Mute to lie there
Meek and still
On the altar
Lie until
All God's plan
He should fulfill
O my soul
Like Isaac be
True submission
All to Thee

O my soul
Like Mary be
Called to bear
Divinity
Shame, reproach
Refuse she may
Silent as He
Has His way
In the balance
All to weigh
Waiting as
He molds the clay
O my soul
Like Mary be
All accepting
Trustingly
O my soul
Like Jesus be
Lamblike through
Eternity
Bound by cords
Of love divine
Saying "Thy will,
Never Mine"
Always ready
To resign
Everything
To His design
O my soul
Like Jesus be
Crucifixion
Willingly

O my soul
Forever be
To thy self
Severity
Selfish ways
Whims forego
Inner fetters
Not to show
Unprotesting
Ever low
To my will
Eternal "No"
O my soul
Forever be
Chained to
Heaven
One with Thee

Submit yourselves
therefore to God.
James 4:7 KJV

The Weeper

One stopped to weep
And watched the bitter tears of sorrow
Fall to earth and form a little pool
In which he saw himself

Then Jesus came
And quickly kneeling down
He traced one word upon it

Compassion

And Marah's waters by that touch
Were made so pure and sweet
That others came to drink their fill
From now a living spring
And went away refreshed

And as they drank
The weeper too had quenched his thirst

And He will
guide them
to springs
of
living water;
and God
will
wipe away
every tear
from their eyes.
Revelation 7:17 RSV

Empty Hands

The more I long to bring my King
Of jewels rare
Of flowers fair
Of proofs of all my love and care
I find I have not anything

I'd thought the gift could surely be
A talent fine
A work of mine
Or something that would be a sign
Of heart's intent and loyalty

But as I searched my treasure hoard
And looked within
I found but sin
And wished that much had never been
For nought I am could please my Lord

For all there was that I could see
Were guilt, sin's stain,
Another's reign
A nature that has caused Him pain
And great need of humility

And so with empty hands I stand
Before His throne
Bereft, alone
With nothing of my very own
But simply there at His command

And as I wonder what shall be
With loving eyes
He bids me rise
And contemplate His sacrifice
And then at last I came to see

Hands empty must be to receive
For lo my King
Has much to bring
He longs to give me everything
Far more than I could dare believe

Such treasures rare are given me
His mercy, grace
His warm embrace
The joy of gazing on His face
All in exchange for poverty

O what a King such love to mete
Who from His store
Pours more and more
O ransomed one, come and adore
And find your treasure at His feet

We are
. . .
as
having
nothing,
and yet
possessing
everything.
2 Corinthians 6:8,10 RSV

The Follower

Where does He go?
Now see Him pass
His footsteps mark
The living grass

Onward He leads
What can I do?
Follow You, Lord
All my life through

By limpid pools
Falls of white lace
Streams of pure joy
Torrents of grace

Deep shaded vales
Portents of dread
Through trackless wastes
No signs ahead

Verdant low hills
Pastures of grain
Sunshine and shade
Refreshing rain

At times through clouds
Gray curling mists
That hide the brink
Of precipice

Up mountain heights
Air pure and clear
Stars within reach
Heaven so near

Waterless plains
Fierce blazing sun
Fainting with thirst
Almost undone

Listen, a lark!
Then sings a dove
Lifting the heart
Tokens of love

Sharp edged stones
Bruising the feet
Painful the way
Tempting retreat

Flowers whose scent
Perfumes the air
Sweetens the days
Saves from despair

Some nights so dark
Scarcely I see
Footprints alone
All that lead me

Coming at last
To Calvary's hill
Seeing a cross
Lonely and still

Still on He goes
Showing the way
Follow thou Me
Cost what it may

Beloved form,
I follow on
Tracing the steps
Where You have gone

O give me grace
Till journey's end
Hold fast my hand
Beloved Friend

It is these
who follow
the Lamb
wherever
He
goes.
Revelation 14:4 RSV

The Ruined Castle

With key in hand through endless rooms I pace,
No footprints but my own have left a trace
On dusty floors, no sun's pure lucent rays
Have filtered through the gloom and darksome haze.

Thick doors and walls protect my soul within,
Barred, locked, from time long past (and from my sin),
The cobwebbed corners tell of disarray,
Of long lost dreams and hopes that would not stay.

The mirrored walls my self alone reveal,
The patterns endless that around me reel,
I drown in images I rather would not see,
My dreams but nightmares are to torture me.

So when I heard that knock upon my gate,
I longed to go, but found I hesitate,
This castle grim is all I've known for years,
And safer is within in spite of fears.

Yet on I go, impelled by unknown grace
To turn the key and look into the face
Of One with Whom I never thought to deal,
Or dreamed that He would come my life to heal.

And as the door creaks open to the air,
The gloom, the past, the anguish and despair
Go rushing out to lose themselves afar,
And in their place has come the Morning Star.

And now I see with untold new delight,
The day has come and swept away the night,
My heart a palace now wherein I sing,
Because it is the lodging of the King.

Fling windows wide and deeply drink the air
The Son of heaven gives me as my fare,
For from my ruins I am set apart,
The Morning Star has risen in my heart.

I,
Jesus,
have sent
My angel
to give you
this testimony
. . .
I am
the Root
and
the Offspring
of David,
and
the bright
Morning
Star.
Revelation 22:16 NIV

Transformation

He led me to the thorns and said,
"My child, I have in store for you
A gift. Take these, embrace them now
And firmly press them close to you."
I shrank and said, "But Lord, there is
No one on earth to truly see
The dread and fear, the pain so deep,
The agony this is for me."

He spoke and told me of His love,
That He full well did know the pain,
He understood, He chose this way
For me to walk and thereby gain
A glimpse of what His own life was,
His sorrows, pain, His toil, His tears,
So far beyond my earthly ken
And thus at last I lost my fears,
And as I took them in my arms
And crushed them to me close, and so,
Gasped with the pain, saw blood run down,
Sank to my knees with head bowed low.

And then a fragrance from them rose,
It seemed that flowers filled the air,
And looking down I saw the thorns
Were whitest lilies, pure and fair,
Their scent an offering from my heart
Ascending to His throne above,
Receiving it the Lord then turned
And spoke to me in words of love,

"The thorns were Mine a while ago
To ease your path, to help you know
That only this way can I bless
And lead you into holiness,

So take My hand and bow your knee
And thorns will precious come to be,
Your heart will lift in joy and sing,
So honored are you by your King,
And this will draw you close to Me
In ways your self could never see,
We will be one when I am through
With all that I have planned for you."

Rejoice
that you participate
in the sufferings
of Christ,
so that
you may be
overjoyed
when
His glory
is revealed.
1 Peter 4:13 NIV

Patmos

Alone he stood — on that forsaken shore
And slowly gazed about —
God's great exile
Before him lay a bleak and hostile land
Behind there stretched the gray forbidding sea
No place to turn, to run, to hide
From what might yet befall

Alone he stood — his tender heart was full
For stripped he was of all
By that Great Hand
All lay in shreds behind that lonely form,
His loves, affinities, his brethren, kin,
Removed from even good that served
To tie him to this earth

And still he stood — and pondered mysteries
Of God's design and will
His destiny
Unknown except to God's great master plan
Unable to do more than cast himself
Soul, spirit, body, heart and will
Into the Love of God

And yet he stood — completely unaware
Of how he seemed to be
So like the Lamb
Whom he had followed, served, and still adored,
Submissive, uncomplaining, meek and mild,
With one great burning flame within
To do his Father's will

Alone he stood — not knowing that this path
So desolate would lead
To death then life

To fall as dead, prone at his Master's feet
When he had gazed upon that blessed Face
And then be raised to enter in
The Lord's new perfect day

Alone he stood – judged worthy to be brought
To heaven's door where yet
No man had stood
Immersed in Jesus had he so become
Completely subject to that Face, that Voice,
That found he now his King to be
Alone his All in all

Alone he stood – oh blessed Hand that took
And separated him
To God alone
O blessed John who grasped that Hand of love
Responding to the cry from God's own Heart
He entered, found his rest within
The Heart of God

I,
John
. . . was
on the island
of Patmos
because of
the word
of God
and the
testimony
of Jesus.
Revelation 1:9 NIV

INDEX

INDEX
continued